TASTEFUL SOUTHERN DELIGHTS OF FAVORITE RECIPES FROM MADEAR'S KITCHEN

PATRICIA MUSTIFUL-JAMES

Genre Library Solutions

Tasteful Southern Delights of Favorite Recipes from Madear's Kitchen by Patricia Mustiful-James

Copyright © 2024 by **Patricia Mustiful-James**

All rights reserved. No part of this book may be reproduced, transmitted, or distributed in any form by any means, including, but not limited to, recording, photocopying, or taking screenshots of parts of the book, without prior written permission from the author or the publisher. Brief quotations for noncommercial purposes, such as book reviews, permitted by Fair Use of the U.S. Copyright Law, are allowed without written permissions, as long as such quotations do not cause damage to the book's commercial value. For permissions, write to the publisher, whose address is stated below.

E-book: 979-8-3304-6185-1
Paperback: 979-8-3304-6186-8
Hardback: 979-8-3304-6187-5

Printed in the United States of America.

Genre Library Solutions
300 Delaware Ave. Suite 210,
Wilmington, DE 19801
www.genrelibrarysolutions.com
(315) 367-7314

DEDICATION MEMORIES

This cookbook is dedicated to Jannie R. Johnson Mustiful, the one who taught me how to cook at an early age. Mother, or Madear as we lovingly call her, used to say that we needed to learn how to cook at a young age. As adults, we would be able to prepare a home cooked meal for our own families one day. Mother did not use recipes; she just told us what ingredients and how much to put into a dish. She cooked by memory.

Baking with my mother became special for me. I learned how to bake my first cake at eight years old. Mother told me all of the ingredients to use, step by step. The cake came out so delicious and I have been baking and cooking seems like forever. A beautiful coconut cake started my cooking career. Now, God has blessed me to put these dishes in writing for all to use.

Others who have been inspirational in my life are …my daughters, my siblings, family, in-laws, and friends near and far. I am blessed to have people in my life who have encouraged me to move forward. The memories of my husband, Keith James, will never fade. He was my inspiration and loved my cooking.

I give the utmost praise to my Lord and Savior, Jesus Christ for all the blessings He has bestowed upon me from day one. I pray that you will enjoy these recipes.

Patricia Mustiful-James

"GOD IS GOOD ALL THE TIME, AND ALL THE TIME GOD IS GOOD"

FORWARD

Cooking is an especially crucial factor in the lives of many who were raised in the rural parts of Louisiana. Patricia (Pat) Mustiful-James is a prime example of a young lady who cherished the love and patience her mother exhibited as a strong, Black mother, and wife as she cooked meals each day for her family. Patricia not only sat at her feet, but she also participated in the daily meals by following her mother's instructions on how to measure ingredients, use the right utensils as well as setting the timer on the stove. She did not know at the time that these lessons would be a lifelong lesson for her personal family. She is now a mother and a widower. Her family adores her and loves her cooking. I am proud to have been her roommate at Grambling State University. She is humble and loving to all she meets. I hope that this book and the lessons taught to her by her mother will give each reader and cook, the joy that Patricia had when she realized that this project should not only be for the stove and oven, but in writing so that the world could get the joy in cooking as she did with her mother.

Dr. Jessie Myles McCaa
Published Author/Retired Teacher/Professional School Counselor,
13th District M.B. A. Woman's Auxiliary Director, Shreveport, La.&
Scholarship Specialist

AUTOGRAPH PAGE

"This book is created with love for you."

FROM: _____

TO: _____

Thank you! Feel free to use any recipe.
I know you will be pleased.
God bless you.

SAVORY CORNBREAD DRESSING
SERVES 10-15

INGREDIENTS

3 packs | Cornbread Mix
1 medium | Bell pepper, chopped
1 large | Onion, chopped
½ cup | Celery, chopped
2 large | Eggs
½ stick or 2 tablespoons | Butter
2 teaspoons | Sage
2 teaspoons | Poultry seasoning
1 can | Cream of chicken soup
1 cup | Breadcrumbs, plain
2-3 cups | Chicken gizzards
Salt & Pepper, to taste

1. Preheat oven to 350 degrees.

2. Prepare and bake the cornbread following the instructions on the cornbread mix.

3. While the cornbread is in the oven, cover the chicken gizzards with enough water and boil on top of the stove. The chicken gizzards should take about 1 hour to cook. Make sure they are soft.

4. Sauté' the onion, bell pepper and celery in butter until softened.

5. When the cornbread is ready, crumble it in a large mixing bowl, add the softened vegetables, chicken broth and cream of chicken soup. Mix well.

6. Once the chicken gizzards are done, cut into pieces and fold into the cornbread mixture.

7. Add the eggs and stir, making sure to mix well.

8. Add salt, pepper, sage, and poultry seasoning to taste.

9. Pour the entire mixture into a casserole dish and bake until golden brown for about 1 hour.

TIPS

I personally like Martha White cornbread mix (white). It gives me the best results. For seasoning, you can use Zatarain's Creole Seasoning. Also, make sure to not stir the dressing while it is baking in the oven. You want to check that all the liquid is dissolved out of the dressing before taking it out of the oven. The consistency should be firm but not dried out.

"Taste and see that the Lord is good; blessed is the one who takes refuge in him."
Psalms 34:8a

TURKEY WINGS
SERVES 5-6

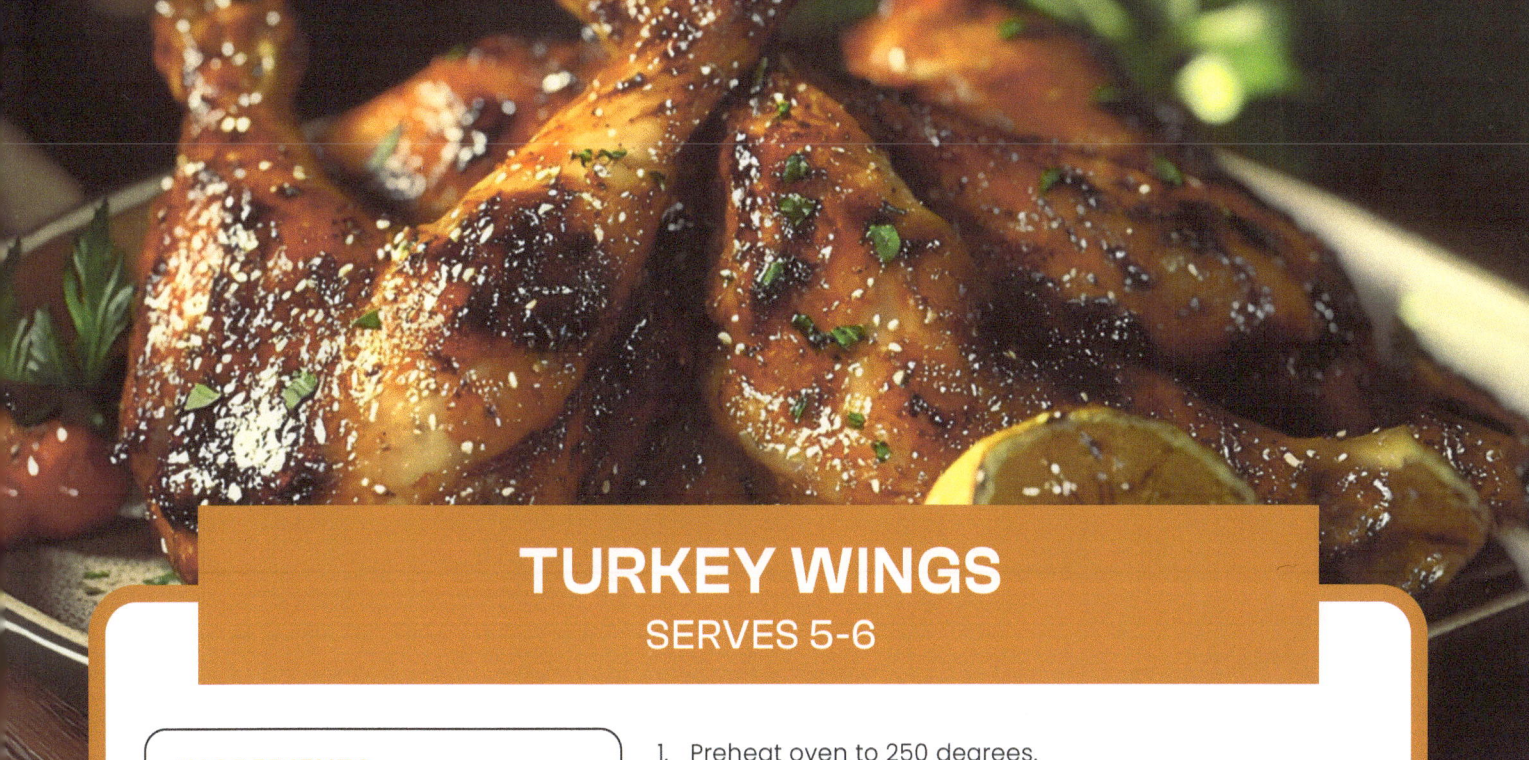

INGREDIENTS

5-6 | Turkey wing parts

2 teaspoons | Garlic seasoning salt

¼ cup | Extra virgin olive oil

Salt & Pepper or your favorite Cajun seasoning, to taste

1. Preheat oven to 250 degrees.
2. Rinse the turkey wings and place in a casserole dish.
3. Pour the olive oil over the turkey wings and set aside.
4. Mix the garlic seasoning, salt, pepper, and Cajun seasoning together in a small bowl.
5. Season the turkey wings with the seasoning mixture.
6. Cover the casserole dish with aluminum foil and bake for 2 hours or until wings are tender.

Preparation is essential in cooking. Make sure that you have everything that is needed for the dish you are getting ready to prepare.

God does the planning; we do the preparing.

God is the one who says (Jeremiah 29:11-13), "For I know the plans I have for you," declares the Lord, "plans to prosper you and not to harm you, plans to give you hope and a future. Then you will call on me and come and pray to me, and I will listen to you. You will seek me and find me when you seek me with all your heart." Notice that God doesn't say, "Let me know when you come up with plans for your future that you want me to bless."

Enjoy this dish!

CHEESY MACARONI & CHEESE
SERVES 10

INGREDIENTS

1-pound box | Elbow macaroni

1 stick | Butter

2-pound bag | Shredded mild cheddar cheese

3 large cans | Evaporated milk

2 tablespoons | Flour

Salt & Pepper, to taste

1. Preheat oven to 350 degrees.

2. Parboil the macaroni, then drain it and place it into a casserole dish.

3. Pour one can of evaporated milk into a bowl and mix with the flour until all lumps are gone.

4. Fold mixture into macaroni, along with the butter. Start adding the rest of the evaporated milk along with 1 bag of mild cheddar cheese. Make sure to stir thoroughly.

5. Layer the remaining bag of the mild cheddar cheese on top of the macaroni mixture. At this point, you can layer as much as you desire. Bake until the cheese on top is melted and bubbly.

Layering our Thoughts

Some meals are easy to prepare, and some are not. Seeing the results of this dish is marvelous. It is simple and to the point. As the finished product is ending, the aroma of this dish makes your mouth crave for a spoonful, but not just yet. The casserole must be topped with the best part, grated cheese.

Psalm 94:11
"The Lord knows all human plans; he knows that they are futile."

MIXED GREENS
SERVES 10-12

INGREDIENTS

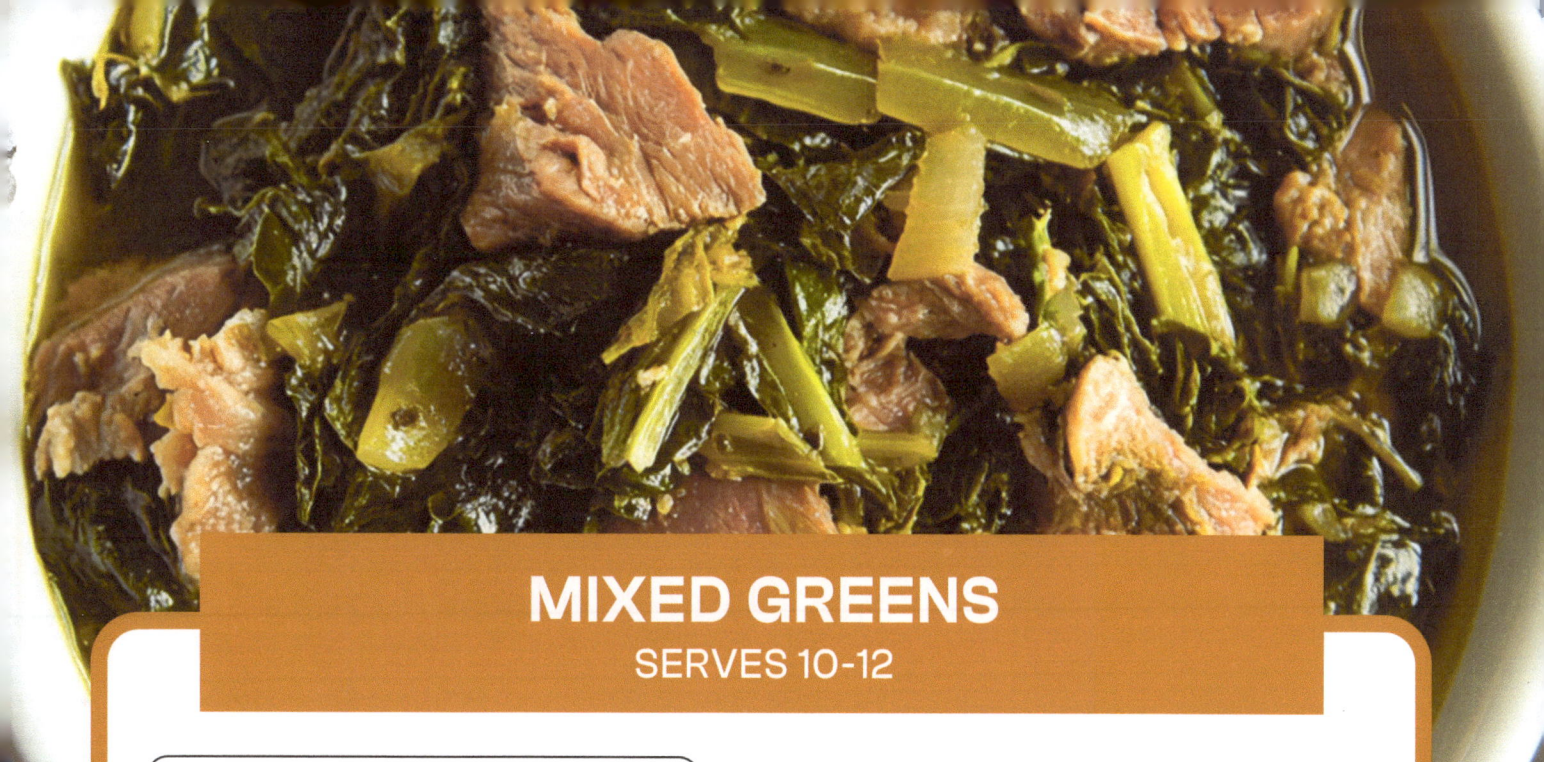

5 bunches | Mustard Greens

5 bunches | Turnip Greens

1 pack | Smoked turkey necks

1 large | Green bell pepper, chopped

1 large | Yellow onion, chopped

1 tablespoon | Minced garlic

2 tablespoons | Extra virgin olive oil

1 | Bay leaf

Salt & Pepper or your favorite Cajun seasoning, to taste

1. Cut and wash the greens thoroughly, making sure to clean the dirt off of the leaves.

2. In a large stock pot, fill with enough water to boil the smoked turkey necks, along with the bell pepper, onion, garlic, olive oil, bay leaf, salt, and pepper.

3. When the turkey necks are tender, add the greens to the stock pot.

4. Cook the greens until tender.

One of my favorite recipes

I am a country girl. This recipe is popular in Southern kitchens. It is simple but creative. The ingredients make it special. My mother would use as many ingredients as possible including two kinds of greens that others did not use in their recipes. Take time to make this your favorite as well. With many mouths to feed, this recipe was filling and there were seconds in the pot. Only God knew that this one dish would nourish us and grow us into the men and women God wanted us to be.

For I know the plans I have for you," declares the Lord, "plans to prosper you and not to harm you, plans to give you hope and a future.
Jeremiah 29:11

UNCLE WALTER'S SWEET POTATOES
SERVES 10-12

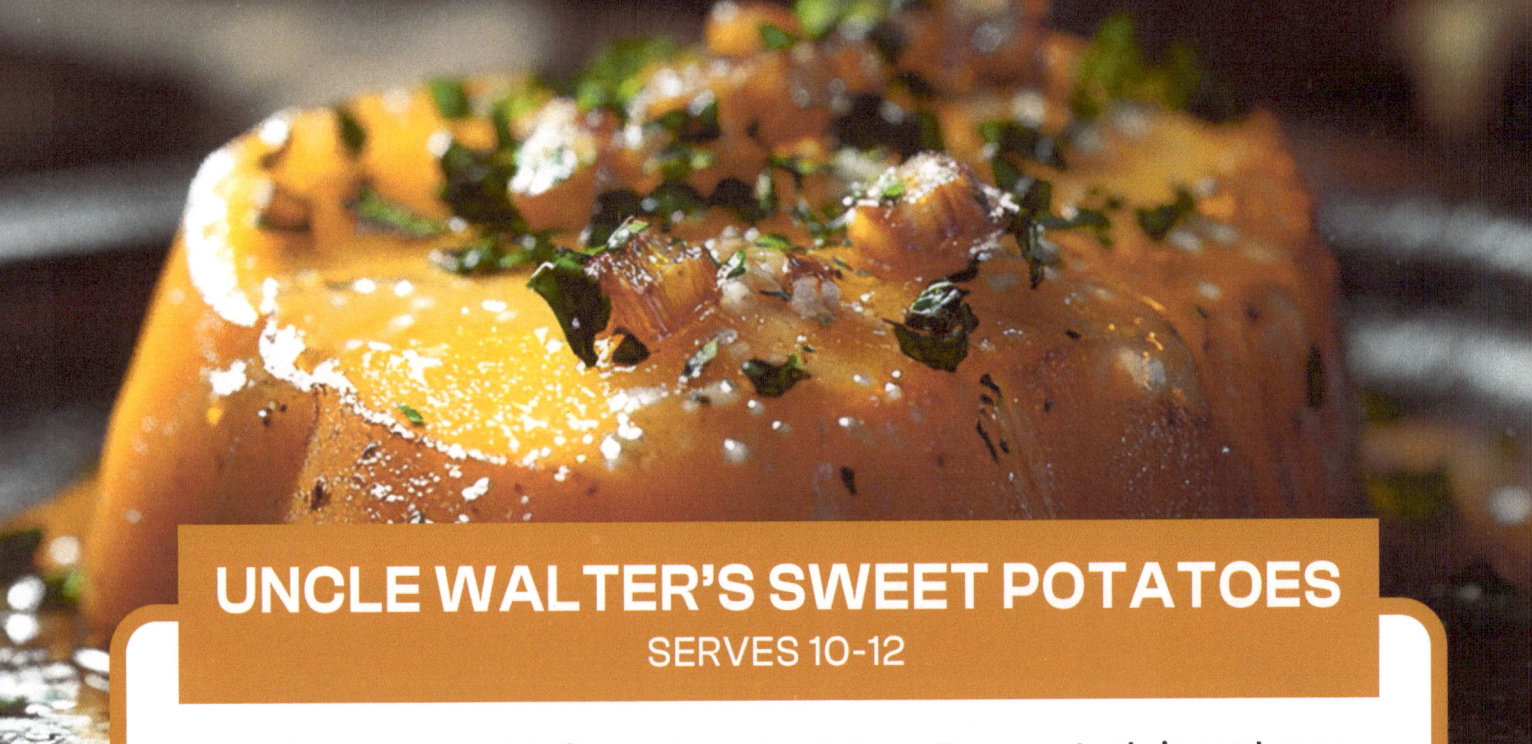

Growing up, we would often eat sweet potatoes. It was a staple in our home. We ate them baked and candied. My Uncle Walter, my daddy's brother, used to visit us often. I recall, during one of Uncle Walter's visits, I was in the kitchen cooking candied sweet potatoes. Uncle Walter told me how to prepare the sweet potatoes. Now, Mother would use cinnamon in her sweet potatoes, but Daddy used to say that using cinnamon was too strong of a spice. Uncle Walter preferred nutmeg because, according to him, it gave the sweet potatoes a better taste. After that, Mother started using nutmeg instead. As time went on, popcorn oil added a different texture to the taste.

INGREDIENTS

- 5-6 large | Sweet Potatoes
- ½ stick | Butter
- 2 cups | Sugar
- 1 tablespoon | Orville Redenbacher Popcorn oil
- 2 teaspoons | Vanilla flavoring
- 2 teaspoons | Nutmeg
- 1 dash | Salt

1. Wash and cut the skin off of the sweet potatoes.
2. Cut the length wise or round, depending on how you like to eat them.
3. Place in large pot and put 1 tablespoon of water, salt, butter, popcorn oil, vanilla, nutmeg, and sugar on top of the sweet potatoes.
4. Cover and cook on medium heat. Make sure not to stir too much once the sweet potatoes get tender.

SoooooooooooooooGood!
This is a great side dish but pairs well with mixed greens and cornbread.
What a dish!

Exodus 23:25
Worship the Lord your God, and his blessing will be on your food and water. I will take away sickness from among you.

DINNER ROLLS
SERVES 15-20

INGREDIENTS

4 cups | All-purpose Flour
1/3 cups | Sugar
1 teaspoon | Salt
1 package | Dry Yeast
1 large | Egg
1/3 cups | Butter, softened
1 ½ cups | Hot water

1. Sift 2 cups of the flour together with the sugar
2. Stir in the yeast.
3. Blend butter into the flour mixture, at a low speed.
4. While the mixer is going, add in the hot water.
5. Add the egg and continue to mix.
6. Add in the remaining flour to make a soft dough.
7. Continue to mix the dough using the dough hook for about 10 minutes or take out of the mixing bowl and knead on a floured board.
8. Place the dough in an oil bowl and cover with a towel to allow the dough to rise, for about 2 hours. The dough should double in size.
9. Once the dough has risen, punch down a bit. The dough can be placed into the refrigerator.
10. When the dough is ready to be baked, shape it into rolls and let it rise a second time.
11. Bake at 375 degrees until browned.
12. Brush melted butter on top when rolls are done.

Just Wait and See!

This is another recipe that requires patience. It is one that has ingredients that will teach us how to wait. One may say, "Why make homemade bread when the stores are loaded with all kinds of bread?" The answer is simple. It is time spent with someone who does not have a degree in culinary arts, nor a Home-Economics degree. This is one recipe that my family loved when done. My mom would make all sorts of rolls, Danishes, brioche, and many more bread recipes.

Matthew 13:33 The Message (MSG)
He told them still another parable: "The kingdom of heaven is like yeast that a woman took and mixed into about sixty pounds of flour until it worked all through the dough."

SEAFOOD GUMBO
SERVES 10-12

INGREDIENTS

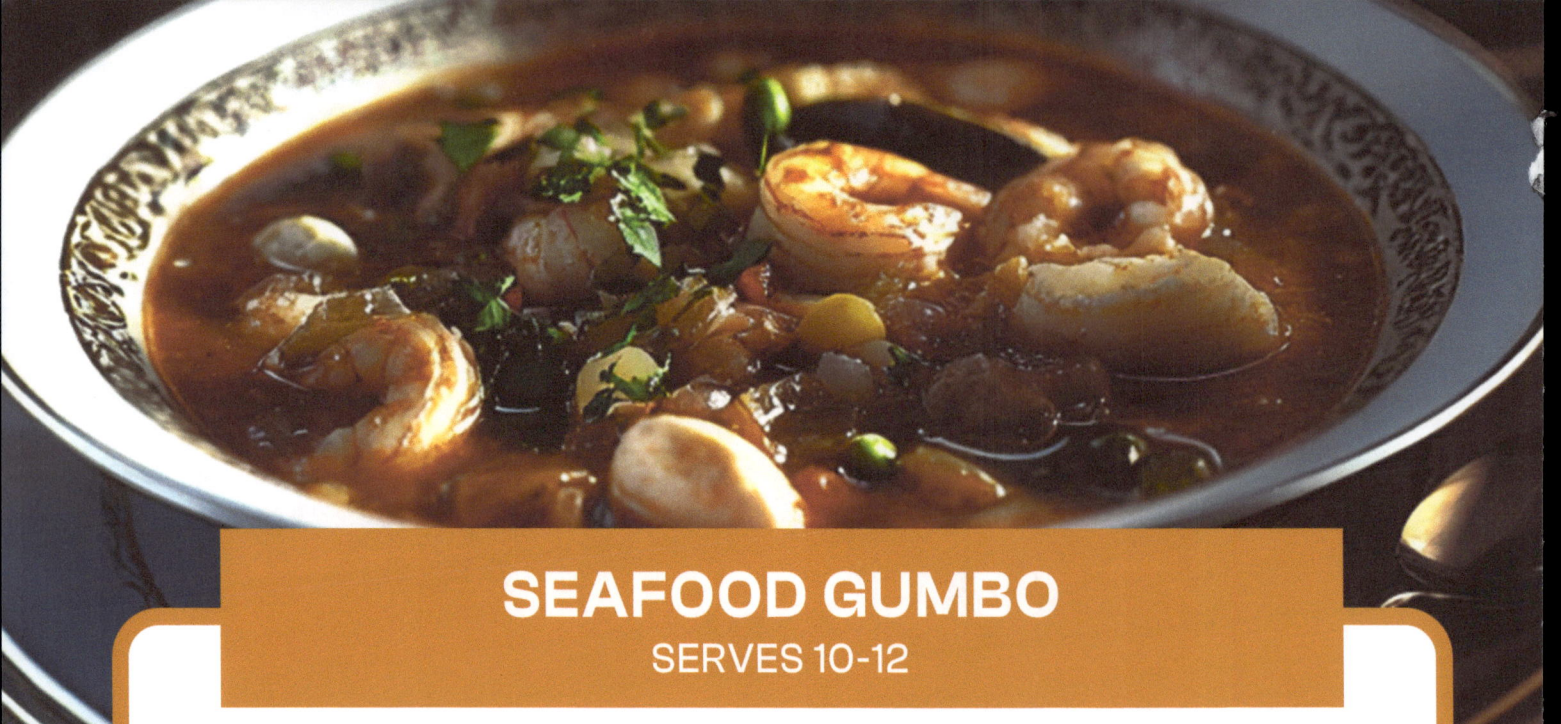

2-3 pounds | Turkey Necks

1 pound | Turkey Smoked Sausage

1-2 pounds | Shrimp

1 pound | Chicken Gizzards

½ pound | Hot Sausage links

2-3 medium | Blue Gumbo Crabs

2 large | Onions(diced)

2 large | Green Bell Peppers (chopped)

2 cups | Celery(chopped)

2 tablespoons | Minced Garlic

½ cup | Minced Parsley

2 pieces | Bay Leaves

1 box | Gumbo Base

½ teaspoon | Black Pepper

½ teaspoon | Crushed Red Pepper flakes

3 cups | Cooked Long Grain Rice

Creole Seasoning, to taste

Gumbo Filet, to garnish

1. Place turkey necks and chicken gizzards and seasonings in the pot and cook until tender. Pre-cook smoke sausages and hot sausages links.

2. Make sure to remove all the extra grease from the links before adding to the rest of the meats.

3. Add the smoke sausages and hot links with the rest of the meats

4. Use the direction from the gumbo base and add that to the meats. (3 cups of water to the gumbo base and stir until all is resolved.

5. Add gumbo crabs and shrimp last to the rest of the meats. Cook until all meats are done, add gumbo filet to garnish. Taste for season

6. Cook rice and drain once done.

7. Serve gumbo on top of rice along with some crackers if you prefer.

A Dish Everyone Enjoys

After getting married, I moved to South Louisiana. My mother-in-law taught me a lot of dishes. One of those was gumbo. Once she showed me all the ingredients that went into making a good gumbo, I made the dish myself. I learned that cooking with a lot of fresh vegetables such as onions, bell peppers, celery (the "holy trinity") and other spices were the key to making a good dish. I also learned that people from South Louisiana cooked differently from the people in North Louisiana. I took on making gumbo for my family doing Thanksgiving time. I choose to only do seafood gumbo, rather than okra or chicken gumbo… and serve it with rice. Everyone loves the dish and I have been asked to make it for a price.

John 4:34
So, when Jesus says in John 4:34, "My food," said Jesus, "is to do the will of him who sent me and to finish his work. Jesus answered, "I am the way and the truth and the life. No one comes to the Father except through me. (John 14:6).

BANANA PUDDING
SERVES 15-20

INGREDIENTS

1 bag Vanilla Wafers (your choice, but I prefer Slaton Homemade cookies)

4 tablespoons flour

½ cup sugar

¼ teaspoon salt

1 lb. bananas (3-4 large)

2 cups scalded milk

2 eggs (separated)

½ teaspoon vanilla

1. Mix flour, ½ cup sugar and salt in top of double boiler; slowly stir in hot milk and cook until mixture thickens, stirring constantly. Stir a little of hot mixture into beaten egg yolks, pour back into double boiler, cook about 2 more minutes. Remove from heat, add vanilla and cool until just warm.

2. Alternate layers of Vanilla Wafers, sliced bananas and pudding in a baking dish. Beat 2 egg whites until foamy, add ¼ cup sugar gradually, beat until stiff. Pile lightly on pudding. Bake in hot (400) oven about 8 minutes or until golden brown.

TIPS

(1) If you want the bananas to not turn brown, you can soak the bananas in a little lemon juice after you slice them. (2) Vanilla wafers get soft over time. If you can find Jack's Vanilla Wafers in your area, they are the best to use because they do not get soft as fast as the traditional Vanilla Wafers.

Psalms 37:15-17
But their swords will pierce their own hearts, and their bows will be broken. Better the little that the righteous have than the wealth of many wicked; for the power of the wicked will be broken, but the Lord upholds the righteous.

BANANA PUDDING/MODERN STYLE

INGREDIENTS

1 large box vanilla instant pudding

3-cup milk (homogenized)

1 can Eagle brand milk

1 small container cool whip (depending on how much you are making, may need two)

2 small cans of crushed pineapples. No juice.

2 cups of chopped pecans

3 or 4 bananas sliced and dipped in lemon juice

2 bags of Jack's vanilla wafers (best)-if not use

1 box vanilla wafers/more if needed.

1. Place instant pudding and milk in a large bowl. Stir until smooth. Then add eagle brand milk and cool whip and stir with a whisk until smooth. Add drained crushed pineapples.

2. Slice bananas and pour lemon juice and let stand for 5 minutes.

3. Line cookies in a casserole dish and dip bananas out of lemon juice and place on top of cookies. Pour pudding mixture over cookies and bananas and continue with it until all cookies, bananas, and pudding mixture. The pudding mixture should cover the pudding. Line the pudding with cookies around the dish. Crush cookies and spread them over the top of the pudding.

If you can find Jack's cookies in your area-use them. They stay firm longer in your pudding.

Enjoy!!

Quickest way, and Just Plain Delicious

My mother never made this quick pudding. She was a beautiful old-school cook. This recipe is extremely easy to make and unbelievably delicious. Some added ingredients were added by my editor. You will be amazed how fast this version will disappear. You may want to make two pans.

Eating together is important. The Bible, in Acts 2:40-47, tells us that sharing meals brings people closer. It changes strangers into friends and makes families feel more connected.

POTATO SALAD

INGREDIENTS

- 6 medium red potatoes, skin off and quartered
- 1 1/2 cups Mayonnaise or Miracle whip
- 1 tablespoon yellow Mustard
- 1/3 cup sweet relish
- Kohler fine salt to taste
- 2 teaspoon sugar
- ¾ teaspoon freshly ground Black pepper
- 5 Boil eggs
- Paprika for garnish

1. Place instant pudding and milk in a large bowl. Stir until smooth. Then add eagle brand milk and cool whip and stir with a whisk until smooth. Add drained crushed pineapples.

2. Place the diced potatoes in a large stockpot and add enough water so that the potatoes ae covered by 1 inch of water along with the eggs. Cook over medium high heat until the water reaches a boil. Then reduce heat to medium to maintain the simmer and continue cooking the potatoes for 5-8 minutes or until the potatoes pierce easily with a fork.

3. Drain the potatoes in a colander. Then return the potatoes to the stockpot and let the potatoes rest until cool enough to manage. Let boil eggs sit in some icy water until ready to put in salad.

4. Once the potatoes are ready to go, add in the mayo, mustard, relish, sugar and salt and pepper to taste. Dice three eggs into the salad. Toss gently until evenly combined.

5. Transfer the potato salad to a serving bowl, slice the remaining eggs into thin slices and place the slices on top of the salad. Garnish with paprika if desired. Cover with some saran wrap and place in refrigerator until ready to serve.

Proverbs 13:10
"Where there is strife, there is pride, but wisdom is found in those who take advice."

As simple as this recipe is, it took my mom a minute or two to complete the dish. She was meticulous about the right measurements of each item to be place in at the right time. Ladies from her church had demonstrated to her when she was growing up how to make a great potato salad. Of course, in her adult age, she added a pinch there until the salad was absolutely delicious. You will love this recipe!

HOMEMADE CORNBREAD

INGREDIENTS

2 cups of white corn meal
1 cup of flour
1 tablespoon baking powder
1 1/2 cup of butter milk
2 eggs
Dash of salt

1. Combine the meal, flour, baking powder and salt together in a medium bowl. Add butter milk and eggs. Stir gently until all ingredients are mixed well.

2. Heat a baking pan or cast-iron skillet (if have) with Olive oil. Once the pan is hot along with the oil, remove the pan and put some of the hot oil in your cornbread mixture. Stir gently and place the cornbread in the hot pan.

3. Bake @ 325 degrees until the bread is golden bread.

TIPS

You will be using this bread to make your cornbread dressing. Sit the bread aside until ready to make your dressing. It is best to make dressing with cool or cold cornbread. You might want to cook cornbread the day before you prepare your dressing.

Many cooks now are going the effortless way to cook cornbread. "I'm so glad that we had no instant cornbread fixes when I was growing up." There is no quick way to make cornbread. This recipe will surprise the novice cook. Go on and make it tonight. Your family will love it.

Proverbs 15:31-33

Whoever heeds life-giving correction will be at home among the wise. Those who disregard discipline despise themselves, but the one who heeds correction gains understanding. Wisdom's instruction is to fear the Lord, and humility comes before honor.

PEACH & PEAR COBBLER
SERVES 15-20

INGREDIENTS

2 cans | Sliced Peaches
1 can | Sliced Pears
1 stick | Unsalted Butter
3 boxes | Pie Crust
2 cups | Sugar
2 teaspoons | Vanilla flavoring
1 dash | Salt

1. Pour peaches and pears into a large pot, along with the juices in the can.

2. Stir in sugar, butter and a dash of salt and cook on medium heat until fruit is cooked down.

3. Roll out one pie crust dough and cut it into squares.

4. Drop each square into the cooking peaches and pears. The pie crust dough will thicken the mixture. The consistency should be a bit firm.

5. Add in the vanilla flavoring.

6. Pour the mixture into a casserole dish or pan.

7. Use the remaining crust to put on top of the fruit mixture. You can decorate it in a basket weave pattern.

8. Once the pie is covered with the pie crust, use a fork or your fingers to decorate around the edges of the pie.

9. Brush some melted butter on top, then sprinkle on a little sugar.

10. Put in the oven and back at 350 degrees until crust is golden brown.

This recipe has become one of my favorites. Who does not enjoy a good home-made peach cobbler thar topped with vanilla ice cream? My family was anxious to come home after church for all the food, but the dessert was just out of this world.

**Psalm 34:8.
King James Version. "Taste and see that the Lord is good; blessed is the one who takes refuge in him."**

**All I can say about this recipe "Yum! Yum!"
Enjoy!**

OLD FASHIONED POUND CAKE
SERVES 15-20

INGREDIENTS

1 cup | Unsalted Butter (2 sticks, softened)
½ cup | Crisco Shortening
3 cups | Sugar
5 large | Eggs
3 cups | Cake Flour
1 teaspoon | Baking Powder
1 cup | Milk
1 teaspoon | Vanilla Flavoring
1 teaspoon | Lemon Flavoring

1. Cream butter, shortening and sugar in a large mixing bowl.
2. Gradually beat until light and fluffy.
3. Add eggs one at a time. Beat well after each egg.
4. Combine flour and baking powder and then add cream mixture, alternating with milk. Mix well after each addition.
5. Stir in vanilla and lemon flavoring.
6. Pour batter in greased and floured Bundt pan.
7. Bake at 350 degrees for 1 hour, 15 minutes or until cake is golden brown.

Growing up in Pelican, LA, we lived in a small community. In those days, Black churches stayed in church all day. Since we were in church all day, Mother would prepare lunch boxes out of shoe boxes. She would line our shoe boxes with wax paper. In our shoe boxes would be fried chicken, sandwiches made with luncheon meat and bologna, and sometimes sweet potato pie. Most importantly, we always had pound cake in our shoe box. That is the one reason I love pound cake, I hope after reading this story, you will love this recipe.

1 Thessalonians 5:16-18.
Rejoice always, pray continually, give thanks in all circumstances; for this is God's will for you in Christ Jesus.

SWEET POTATO PIE
SERVES 15-20

INGREDIENTS

2 large | Sweet Potatoes
1 stick | Unsalted Butter
6 large | Eggs
2 cups | Sugar
1 cup | Evaporated Milk
2 teaspoons | Vanilla Flavoring
2 packages | Pie Crust
1 dash | Salt

1. Wash and peel sweet potatoes. Cut it up in pieces, put in water, and bring to a boil.
2. Boil potatoes until completely soft.
3. Pour off water and put the potatoes into a large mixing bowl.
4. Beat in butter, sugar, and a dash of salt. Mix well.
5. Stir in eggs, one at a time.
6. Add milk and vanilla. At this point, the mixture should not be too soupy but a consistency and thickness of apple sauce.
7. Pour the mixture into the pie crust shell.
8. Bake at 325 degrees until done.

TIPS

(1) Sometimes when beating the sweet potato mixture, there will be small fibrous strings. Make sure you take out all of the strings from the mixture. Most of the fibers will come out on the beaters when mixing. (2) Taste the mixture as you go along to make sure it is sweet enough to your liking. If not, add more sugar. (3) To keep the edges of the pie crust from burning or getting too dark before the pie is thoroughly cooked, cover the edges with foil before you start baking the pie.

Psalm 18:32.
"It is God who arms me with strength and keeps my way secure."

This is one of my favorites. I may have failed to say that we raised most of our food. The land was great for planting and food grew exceedingly well. Sweet potatoes grew so well that we shared them with our neighbors and friends.
What a blessing to share or love.

EGG NOG
SERVES 15-20

INGREDIENTS

6 large | Eggs
1 can | Condensed Milk
2 cups | Sugar
½ gallon | Milk
1 dash | Nutmeg

1. Separate egg whites from egg yolks.
2. Put egg yolks in a stock pot and add sugar and milk, stirring constantly and vigorously.
3. Add the condensed milk.
4. Continue stirring mixture until it starts to boil.
5. Beat egg whites until fluffy.
6. Add the egg white mixture to the pot once it boils.
7. When ready to drink, sprinkle a dash of nutmeg on top and enjoy.

Hebrews 13:16
And do not forget to do good and to share with others, for with such sacrifices God is pleased.

This is a shared beverage for all who arrive at our house for Thanksgiving and Christmas. The family loves this drink whether for breakfast or any meal of the day. The only thing is, my mother-in-law's Egg Nog is better than store bought Egg Nog.

EASY BROCCOLI RICE CASSEROLE

INGREDIENTS

2 Cups of rice

1 stick of butter

1 can mushroom soup

2 pkgs Broccoli (cut up) fresh Broccoli is fine

1 lb. Velveeta cheese

Salt and pepper to taste

Cook rice and broccoli separately until half done. Remove from heat and combine cooked rice and steamed broccoli, butter, and mushroom soup. Mix well and add cheese. Layer cheese. Cook 350 degrees for about 1 hour.

Whoever is patient has great understanding, but one who is quick-tempered displays folly.
Proverbs 14:29

This verse is a perfect example of how my mother taught us. With ten children under one roof, there was bound to be some disagreements from time to time. Yet, we knew how far to go. Our parents did not "fuss" in front of us at all. They were examples for our family and the community. God bless them both for the legacy they left. Something as simple as this recipe brought joy to my mother when she cooked this dish for her family.

Each of you should give what you have decided in your heart to give, not reluctantly or under compulsion, for God loves a cheerful giver.
2 Corinthians 9:7

CORNISH HENS

INGREDIENTS

- 2 Cornish hens about 1.5 pound each
- 3 tablespoons olive oil divided
- 1 teaspoon Zatarain Creole seasoning or 1 teaspoon kosher salt to taste
- ½ teaspoon black pepper
- ½ teaspoon lemon zest
- ¼ teaspoon thyme leaves
- ¼ parsley flakes
- ¼ teaspoon garlic powder
- ¼ teaspoon mince garlic
- 1 onion
- 1 bell pepper

1. Arrange the hens in a large casserole dish or on a rimmed baking sheet. Brush the hens with olive oil. Twist wings to tuck under the bird. Season hens with all the seasoning: Zatarain or salt, black pepper, lemon zest, thyme leave, garlic powder and garlic.

2. Chop onions and bell pepper. Place inside of the hens. Cover with foil and bake 55-65 minutes or just until hens are brown and tender.

3. Cut the hens in half and serve.

Genesis 9:3 - Everything that lives and moves about will be food for you. Just as I gave you the green plants, I now give you everything.

For some of you modern cooks, you probably go to the grocery store to buy Cornish hens, smoked or the ones that are two in a package. Buying Cornish hens was not in my mom's vocabulary. We raised chickens. They were a delicacy the way my mother cooked them. Today, everything is microwaved ready. We were not reared with a microwave cooking or warming our food. I do not think that young people would survive without a microwave or fast foods. Thank God for homemade dishes straight from the yard.

QUICK SAUSAGE JAMBALAYA
SERVES 4

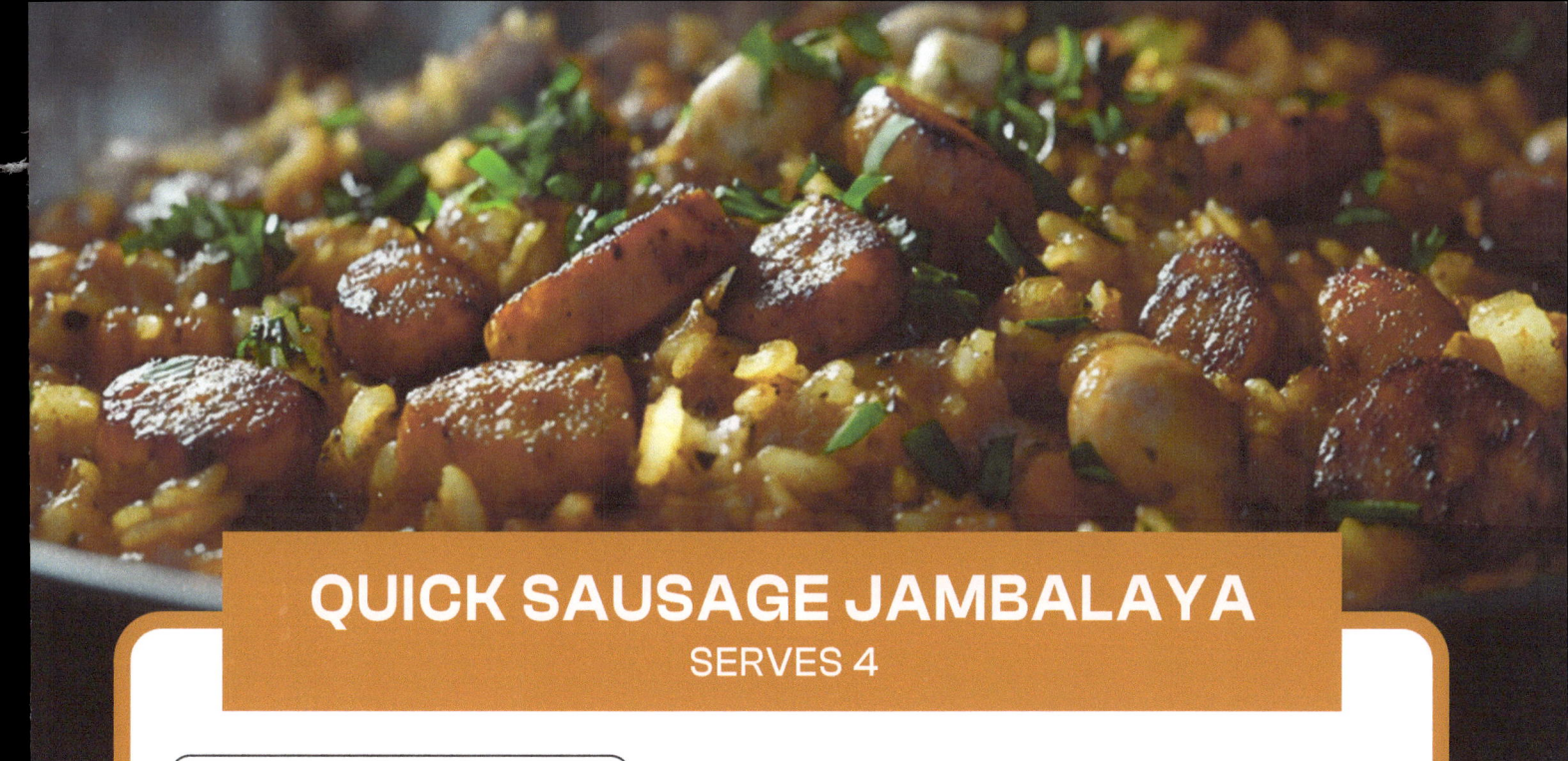

INGREDIENTS

- 3.5oz bag Success white rice
- 1/2lb. Smoked turkey sausage, sliced
- ½ cup chopped onion
- ½ cup chopped green bell pepper.
- 14.5 can Del Monte Cajun Stewed tomatoes, un-drained
- 1 Tbs Creole seasoning

Cook rice according to package directions, drain. Cook sausage, onion and green pepper in a medium saucepan until sausage is brown. Stir in tomatoes, Creole seasoning and rice. Cook over medium heat, stirring often, until thoroughly heated.

Jambalaya has influences in Spanish, French, African, Native American and Caribbean cooking styles and produce. Unlike seafood gumbo, it is mostly Spanish due to the dish's similarity to Paella, which was brought to New Orleans. Once it came to Louisiana and its rich cooking styles. It was perfected in every Black home. No one dish was the same. This is how my mother in-law did her original style. Jambalaya is like sharing the love of God to everyone. My mother was notorious for sharing her cooking not only to family, but neighbors and those in need. It reminds me of Jesus feeding the 5000. She showed love just as Jesus did to the people, he fed.

Mark 6:37-44
But he answered, "You give them something to eat". They said to him, "That would take more than half a year's wages! Are we to go and spend that much on bread and give it to them to eat"? "How many loaves do you have? He asked. "Go and see". When they out, they, "Five-and two fish". Then Jesus directed them to have all the people sit down in groups on the green grass. So they sat down in groups of hundreds and fifties. Taking the five loaves and two fish and looking up to heaven, he gave thanks and broke the loaves. Then he gave them to his disciples to distribute to the people. He also divided the two fish among them all. They all ate and were satisfied, and the disciples picked up twelve basketfuls of broken pieces of bread and fish. And they that did eat of the loaves were about five thousand men.

DIRTY RICE

INGREDIENTS

1 (14-OUNCE) can chicken broth

1 bay leaf

1 celery rib, chopped

1 ½ cups long-grain rice

1 tablespoon bacon grease or vegetable oil

½ pound ground turkey

½ pound pork sausage

1 medium onion, chopped

1 celery rib, chopped

½ green bell pepper, seeded and chopped

2 cloves garlic, minced

½ teaspoon salt

2 teaspoons Cajun seasoning, I like Zartarian

¼ teaspoon dried thyme

1. Set aside ½ cup of chicken broth and pour remaining chicken broth in a medium saucepan. Add 1 ½ cups of water and bay leaf. Bring it to boil. Add rice, cover, and cook 20 minutes

2. Heat oil in a cast iron Dutch oven (if have, you can use any type of skillet). Add ground turkey and pork sausage and crumble with a wooden spoon.

3. Once you have the meats crumbled, add onion, celery, and green pepper. Cook stirring occasionally until meats are no longer pink and vegetables are softened. Add garlic and continue to cook for 5 minutes.

4. Add salt, Cajun seasoning, and thyme.

5. Add reserved chicken broth and scrape the bottom of the pan to release all the brown pieces. Let simmer for 1 minute.

6. Remove bay leaf from rice and add rice to Dutch oven. Stir it into the ground turkey mixture. Keep the heat o while you stir. Once it is combined well, remove from the heat.

Proverbs 15:17
Better a small serving of vegetables with love
than a fattened calf with hatred.

Do you receive the concept?

BLACK-EYE PEAS

INGREDIENTS

1-pound frozen black eye peas

1 cup smoke sausage or turkey

4-5 thick bacon slices

1 large onion, diced

1 stalk celery, diced

2-3 teaspoons minced garlic

1 jalapeno, minced (optional) replace with cayenne pepper

2 teaspoons fresh thyme, minced

Bay leaf

¼ cup Olive oil

1-2 teaspoons creole seasoning

7-8 cups chicken broth

Salt and pepper to taste

1. Add beans olive oil and smoke season turkey to a large pot covering with 3-4 inches of hot water on a medium flame and bring to boil.

2. In a large skillet, sauté chopped bacon until brown and crispy about 4-5 minutes, then add sausage sauté for about 2-3 more minutes. Remove bacon and sausage mixture, set aside.

3. Throw in the onions, celery, garlic, jalapenos, thyme and bay leaf and salute for about 3-5 minutes, until onions are wilted and aromatic,

4. Then pour in the chicken broth

5. Add more stock or water if the mixture becomes dry ad thick, the texture of the beans should be thick, creamy but not watery.

6. Taste and adjust for seasonings with pepper, creole seasoning and salt if needed. Serve over cooked rice and garnish with green onions.

Genesis 1:29
Then God said, "I give you every seed-bearing plant on the face of the whole earth and every tree that has fruit with seed in it. They will be yours for food.

God has always been good!
He is blessing us right now.
Enjoy this recipe!
I love these peas!

CABBAGE

INGREDIENTS

1 head of cabbage

Smoke ham hocks or smoke turkey parts

2 tablespoon unsalted butter

2 tablespoon olive oil

½ teaspoon salt

Fresh black pepper to taste

2-3 cut red potatoes(peeled)

1/1/2-2 cups chicken broth

1. Slice cabbage into quarters, removing & discarding the hard stem at the center. Slice each quarter into 1-inch-wide strips. Set it aside.

2. In a large pot, melt the butter and add olive oil. Cook ham hocks and turkey parts until tender, then add remaining ingredients to the pot, including the cabbage.

3. Stir and bring to a boil, immediately reduce heat to a simmer, and cover.

4. Simmer 12-15 minutes or until cabbage is tender to your liking. (Do not overcook or cabbage will be slimy)

5. Taste and adjust seasoning if needed.

Serve it with cornbread and sweet potatoes for double good luck for the coming new year.

Adding potatoes into cabbage gives them a kick.

Psalm 23

The Lord is my shepherd, I lack nothing. He makes me lie down in green pastures, he leads me beside quiet waters, he refreshes my soul. He guides me along the right paths for his name's sake. Even though I walk through the darkest valley, I will fear no evil, for you are with me; your rod and your staff, they comfort me. You prepare a table before me in the presence of my enemies. You anoint my head with oil; my cup overflows. Surely your goodness and love will follow me all the days of my life, and I will dwell in the house of the Lord forever.

The 23rd book of Psalms was a regular recital for us at bedtimes. We said our prayers and the 23rd Psalm. This has been a regular for my children as well. Lessons learned as children never go away. I can still hear my mother reciting the verses while cooking. What a blessing for the food and the eaters. The food was blessed before we arrived at the table.

BAKED CHICKEN

INGREDIENTS

4-6 Chicken thighs
(your preference part of the chicken)

4 teaspoon garlic powder

Cilantro

Zatarain Creole seasoning
(your preference)

1. Preheat oven to 375 degrees F (190 degrees C)

2. Place foil in baking dish and lay thighs on the foil. Season chicken thighs on all sides with garlic powder, Cilantro, and seasoning. Cover the pan with foil and bake chicken in the preheated oven until it is no longer pink at the bone and the juices run clear, about 30 minutes.

**Now he who supplies seed to the sower and bread for food will also supply and increase your store of seed and will enlarge the harvest of your righteousness.
II CORINTHIANS 9:10**

May God Bless You.

Patricia Mustiful-James